# Experiencing the Prophetic Flow of God

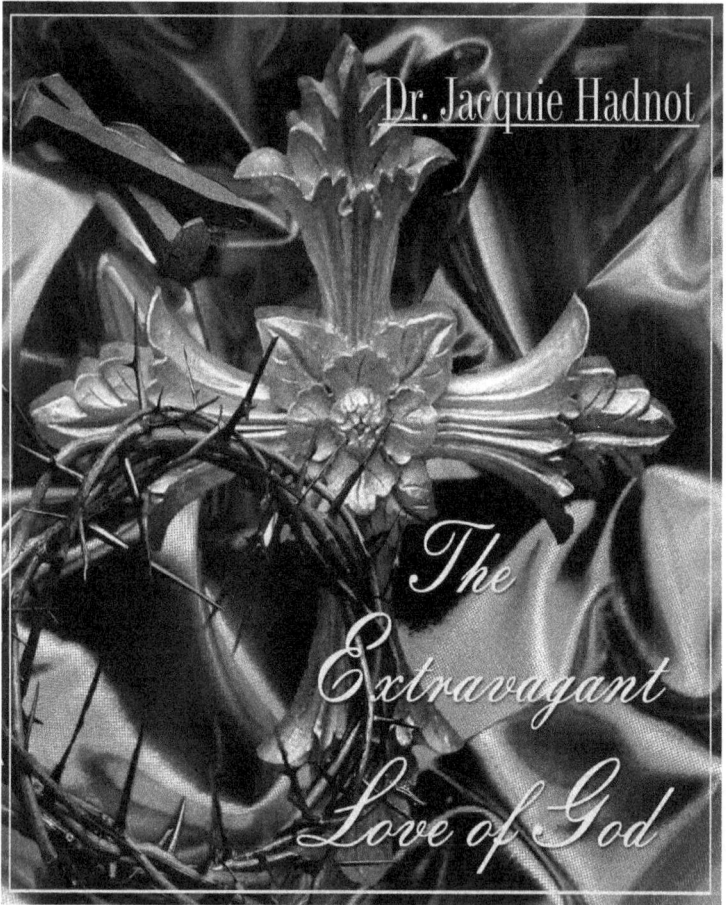

## Dr. Jacquelyn Brown-Hadnot

# **Dedication**

This book is dedicated to My Lord and Savior Jesus Christ.  Thank you for the extravagant love that you shower on me.

To everyone with a desire for more intimacy with God.

To every minister of the Gospel who has given their life to spreading the uncompromising message of Jesus Christ and His precious gift to us.

This book is dedicated to every one that lives and breathes, "The kingdom of heaven suffers violence and the violent take it by force." Matthew 11:12.

This book is also dedicated to everyone who has been a part of It Is Written Ministries, Igniting the Fire Media Group and GLORI Radio.

# Acknowledgements

I am blessed to have an awesome Man of God in my life, my best friend, Minister Gregory Hadnot.  It is such a joy to have a spouse who believes in me and allows me to flow in the ways the Lord has called me.  I thank the Lord for your encouragement and support through this journey.  Thank you for being my "Pa Pa" and my best friend.

To my daughter, Jacquanda, and my grandson Tristan.  I am so blessed to have you both in my life.  You bring me so much joy and words cannot express the love I have for you.  Jacquanda, watching you grow into such a beautiful woman is the greatest joy a mother can experience.  Thank you for being the second best thing I have ever done in my life.  Tristan, you are the best grandson "Mama J" can have.  I love you both so much.

To Dr. Margaret Wright for being my friend. Thank you for being "Elijah" and showing me what it means to walk in the office of a Prophet called by God.

To Michael Reese, Zenobia Smith, Art Toombs, Jonathan Strother and Jimmy Brown, for the friendship and the sweet music we have birthed together.

# Table of Contents

| | | |
|---|---|---|
| Dedication | | |
| Acknowledgements | | |
| Foreword | | |
| Welcome | | |
| Introduction | | 8 |
| Chapter 1 | Reaching for the Fullness of God | 13 |
| Chapter 2 | Surface Christianity | 21 |
| Chapter 3 | The Sacrifice for Deeper | 23 |
| Chapter 4 | What does it mean to seek the Lord? | 27 |
| Chapter 5 | What Is True Worship? | 31 |
| Chapter 6 | A Prepared Place for God | 37 |
| Chapter 7 | The Press | 45 |
| Chapter 8 | Worship in the War | 51 |
| Chapter 9 | The Call to the Five-Fold Ministry | 59 |
| Chapter 10 | Who Is Jesus? | 67 |
| Chapter 11 | What I Learned Through the Valley of... | 71 |
| Chapter 12 | Time Alone with God | 81 |
| Chapter 13 | The Nails He Bore for Us | 91 |
| Chapter 14 | The Extravagance of God's Love | 101 |
| Conclusion | Growing Deeper | 105 |
| | Prayer of Salvation | 111 |
| | About Dr. Jacquie | 114 |
| | Books & Materials | 118 |

# Foreword

All that you thought you knew about worship will be challenged after you experience this CD and book. The entire body of Christ is yearning for a deeper encounter with the Spirit of God and you will definitely not be disappointed when you hear the selection entitled, "Deeper." This is a time when our Lord is awakening the deep love for Him that has been dormant too long.

I encourage you to allow the Spirit of the Living God to minister to you as you hear each selection on this CD and journey through this book. God loves us so much and has proven it repeatedly. Now, I invite you to glean from these pages not only the depth of that love, but a refreshing and restoration of your love towards Him. I pray that you are consumed with "The Extravagant Love of God." Love Him with all you heart, soul, mind and strength; then you can be confident that you are returning to our Lord the extravagant love He deserves. God bless you!

Dr. Margaret Wright, Author & Teacher

# *Welcome to*
# *The Extravagant Love of God:*
# *Experiencing the Prophetic Flow of His Love*

~~~~~~~~~~~~~~~~~~~~~~~~~~~~~~

Jesus, my awesome Lord and Savior, Your name is the sweetest name I know and I want your name to be the first and last name in this book. Lord, I ask in Your name to lead everyone who reads these pages to see You as You are -- Awesome, Powerful, Magnificent, Holy, Righteous, worthy of our worship and our praise. I pray that they come to behold Your beauty and begin to inquire in Your temple. I pray that every Word You have spoken to me will resonate from the pages of this book and ignite a fire for worship in their hearts. I pray all these things in your precious, Holy Name, Jesus. Amen.

## Introduction

~~~~~~~~~~~~~~~~~~~~~~~~~~~~~~~~~~~~

*Seven things you should know before beginning this book:*

1. God is calling us to "Worship Him More."

2. Worship is very important to God.

3. Your victory is in your worship.

4. Worship is simple; it is not complicated or magical.

5. If you don't worship the Lord, you will miss Him.

6. Worship is God's weapon of choice.

7. We worship God for *"who He is"* and not for *"what He has done for us."*

While birthing the music CD the *Extravagant Love of God*, the Lord impressed upon my heart to write this book as an encouragement to His people. This book contains lyrics from the songs on the CD, words of wisdom for His people, and the prophetic Word that He has spoken to me over the years.

I did not question the Lord when He commissioned me to write this book, *"for my thoughts are not your thoughts, neither are your ways my ways," declares the LORD.* (Isaiah 55:8). I believe His purpose for birthing this book is, *"to allow the people a glimpse of Me."* The Lord wants His people to know that He is alive, active, and concerned about our every need. He has not forgotten us; He said he would never leave us nor forsake us.

Within these pages you will find the message the Lord has for His people in these "perilous" end times. I pray that you are blessed by this book because the Lord poured out His heart and desires for His people through our intimate times together. While He is giving instruction, correction, and guidance through this book - it should not take away from your personal time alone with Him. In fact, it is my prayer that this book and music CD will ignite a fire within you for more of His presence, more of His power, and more of His passion in your life.

Several years ago as I was preparing for bed the Lord spoke these words to me. He said, *"The reason you have the relationship with me that you do is because you have chosen to live a life for me. Few people desire to live at this level. This is why I speak to you. It is not a light thing, but it is not enough, go deeper."*

Since that day I have been pressing in to deeper.  In order to go deeper I needed to discover the path necessary for *growing* deeper.  It is not a light thing and it is not an easy thing.  *Deeper* has required a sacrifice unlike any other in my life.  It has required dying to "Jacquie" in ways that cannot be contained within the pages of this book.

The day we ask the Lord to live in us is the day that we must die to our selfish ways.  Our personal agendas must be laid at the foot of the Cross and we must pick up our cross and follow Christ.  Everything about us must change if we are to reach "deeper" and to receive the fullness of God.

As a Prophet of God to His people, the place where God often has me is alone, but not lonely.  Isolated but not forsaken.  Quiet but not shut down.  It would not be possible for me to write this book if I did not live a life that is totally sold out to Him.  Why do I say this?

Because **souls are at stake** and I will not have the blood of souls on my hands because I wrote a book that lead people astray.  Again I say s**ouls are at stake** and the day we wake up and realize that what really matters in the Kingdom of God are the "souls" - then as *the Body* we will begin to change the way we do and view things.

We should not be warehousing people - we are called to set the captives free.  It is sad when I see people in bondage and they believe there is no way out.  They give up or compromise never allowing the Lord to move in their lives.  Hopeless is helpless unless they come to know Jesus Christ.

The objective of this book is to encourage, inspire, motivate and show the people of God that He is alive and speaking to His people in order to lead, guide and direct our paths.  God is talking.  Are you listening?

More love, more power - more of You, Lord in our lives!

*Chapter 1*

## *The Prophetic Word of God*
# Reaching for the Fullness of God

~~~~~~~~~~~~~~~~~~~~~~~~~~~~~~~~~~~~

If we are to receive the fullness of God, we must stop trying to do that which is convenient and easy for us.  In order to receive the extravagance of God's blessings, we must be willing to come out of our comfort zones.

There are times when we make excuses for missing our season because we have allowed the enemy to infiltrate our thoughts and we become incapable of walking out the vision due to fear or doubt.  Because of issues like pride, laziness or lack of heart's desire we miss the blessings of God.  We cannot expect new results if we continue to operate in the same manner.

God wants US to be as extreme for His Kingdom work as we are in other things we have a REAL passion for.  The reason we live such lackluster lives is because our spiritual lives are lackluster.  Do you realize that physically lazy people dishonor themselves, but spiritually lazy people dishonor God?

Example: We will watch twenty hours of television, but only pray twenty minutes. We never stay with a project long enough to see results because we move around from idea to idea or church to church with no stability in our lives. God is never allowed to bless us because we move around like nomads.

God will bless and grow that which is committed to Him. Commitment means staying the course - through snow, rain, heat, disappointment or discouragement. If no one believes in the vision - YOU SHOULD.

## *The Prophetic Word of God*
# People Need to See Victorious Living
~~~~~~~~~~~~~~~~~~~~~~~~~~~~~~~~~~~

While in prayer one evening the Lord said, *"People need to see victorious living. I am going to set you before the people as an example of a victorious life.*

My initial thought was, "Lord, does that mean you are going to put me on display? I don't think I am the person for the job.  Don't you remember all the things I have done in my past?"

I thought of one million reasons why the Lord chose the wrong person.  Who am I to question God?

*The Word of the Lord*

'For I know the plans that I have for you,' declares the LORD, 'plans for welfare and not for calamity to give you a future and a hope. Jeremiah 29:11

## *The Prophetic Word of God*
# Arise to the Fullness of God

~~~~~~~~~~~~~~~~~~~~~~~~~~~~~~~~~~~~~

*For those who seek me as you do they will find a deep treasure in Me.  Many will seek, but few will find Me because they do not live for Me.  The treasure found in a life for Me cannot be compared to anything man will ever know.  Tell My people to seek Me with the whole heart. The glory of My light which I have shown you is available to them also.  I am no respecter of persons.  Tell them of My glory. Tell them of My love. They must know the price*

*I paid.  Trust Me even more for I will perform My word.*

*Talitha Cumi, Daughter Arise! To the purpose and destiny I have set before you before the foundation of the world.  I have called you to be a Prophet to My people. Be strong and trust in Me.  Speak My words to My people. They must know the truth for in the truth they are made free. Tell them to live in My Word and in My presence. Tell them to walk upright before Me.  All I am doing for you I will do for them also.  Daughter, stay in My presence.  Stay in My Word for in them you will find peace.*

*As you asked I have searched your heart, I have tried your reins and tested you in the fire.  As you asked I will show you My glory, but there is more that I require of you.  You must go deeper into Me.  You have only seen a glimpse of My glory.  There is much more for you to see. Trust Me even more.  Although man thinks it strange, you know My power and My glory.  Continue to walk in it.*

*The healing you desire for My people will begin to manifest - be patient.  Know that I am with you and again no good thing will I withhold from you because I love you. Seek Me more in prayer. Feed My sheep and tell them of My love.*

*The Word of the Lord*

## The Prophetic Word of God
# Let God Out of the Box!

~~~~~~~~~~~~~~~~~~~~~~~~~~~~~~

The Lord woke me at 3:00 a.m. with these words, *"Tell My people that I desire to bless them, but how can I bless them if they keep putting Me in a box."* He went on the say that, *"each time we put Him in a box we limit the blessings in our lives."*

The Lord then showed me a huge box – the size of a refrigerator box. He placed me inside of the box and began to tell me about the limits we place on Him when He is inside the box. I was amazed as His meaning was becoming clear to me. The Lord said, *"every time we allow the enemy to come in and we sin against God we block the flow of His blessings."* I then saw myself hitting the inside of the box and with each extension of my hands

I was hindered by the box. I could go no further than the parameters of the box. I was limited in what I could do inside the box.

The Lord showed me that in this same way we limit Him in our lives when we fall prey to the bait of Satan. Our blessings are cut off the minute we succumb to the wiles of the enemy and often we miss our due season. You must let God out of the box if you are going to possess the promises of God.

## *The Prophetic Word of God*
## Seeing the Beauty

~~~~~~~~~~~~~~~~~~~~~~~~~~~~~~~~~~~~~

*There is still beauty in the things I have created. There is joy in the world if you seek Me for it. Even the clouds show My beauty. The enemy hates anything that represents peace, love or joy - for in him there is no peace. When My people give in to the enemy, the world as they know it becomes dark and meaningless. It saddens Me to see My people live this way.*

The Word of the Lord

*One thing I have asked from the LORD, that I shall seek: That I may dwell in the house of the LORD all the days of my life, to behold the beauty of the LORD and to meditate in His temple. Psalm 27:4*

*Your ability to press in to worship determines your level of intimacy with the Lord.*

*Shallow worship equals NO intimacy.*

**Deep calls unto**

# Chapter 2

## The Prophetic Word of God
## Surface Christianity

~~~~~~~~~~~~~~~~~~~~~~~~~~~~~~~~~~~

The Lord spoke one morning as I was beginning a fast. He said, *for far too long My people have been living on the surface of Me.  They know of Me, but they do not know Me."  I want you to go deeper into Me and learn of Me."*

*There is no room for surface Christianity in these last days.  We must go after God with a strong sense of urgency.  The people must go after Me as if it was their last breath - because it just might be.*

*As the outpouring begins many will not know or perceive My move because they are not Mine.  Those who hunger for Me must not look to the church as it has become  - a self glorifying man made system of worship which is often stale and My sweet savor is not present.*

*The people must come to the knowledge of self-will - it stands in opposition to My will and it will keep My people from My fullness. The breaking of self-will can only occur when man seeks to obey Me without question. This will only occur when he learns to trust in Me. Trust comes through faith. Self-will means man trusts himself more than the sovereign hand of God.*

The Lord went on to say, *there are many people who have never tasted victory because they have never tasted Me. They come to you daughter, because you are their example of a victorious life. I told you the ministry [It Is Written Ministries] was a place of refuge for My people.*

The Word of the Lord

# Chapter 3

## The Prophetic Word of God
# The Sacrifice for Deeper

~~~~~~~~~~~~~~~~~~~~~~~~~~~~~~~~~~~

*In order to go deeper, it will require sacrifice.  Do you see the enemy trying to hinder My people as they move into position to advance towards their due season?*

The Word of the Lord

Read & meditate on:

**Psalm 1:3**
*But his delight is in the law of the LORD, And in His law he meditates day and night.  He will be like a tree firmly planted by streams of water, Which yields its fruit in its season And its leaf does not wither; And in whatever he does, he prospers.*

**Jeremiah 17:8**
*For he will be like a tree planted by the water, That extends its roots by a stream And will not fear when the heat comes; But its leaves will be green, And it will not be anxious in a year of drought Nor cease to yield fruit.*

**Psalm 42:7**
*Deep calls to deep...*

**Galatians 6:7-9**
*Let us not lose heart in doing good, for in due time [season] we will reap if we do not grow weary.*

## *The Prophetic Word of God*
# The Anointing to Create

~~~~~~~~~~~~~~~~~~~~~~~~~~~~~~~~~~~~~~~

The anointing to create comes when you can hear the Lord clearly. As you listen for His voice, instructions will flow through your spirit. As He flows through us and we go deeper in Him, His anointing to create will flow through everything we do for Him.

*The anointing to discern the things of God and those not of God comes in the ability to hear Me clearly. Do not allow the enemy to bring discouragement through health or finances. These are areas he is fighting you. Speak to your mountains.*

<div align="right">

The Word of the Lord

</div>

*Bless the LORD, you His angels, Mighty in strength, who perform His word, obeying the voice of His word!  Bless the LORD, all you His hosts, You who serve Him, doing His will.  Bless the LORD, all you works of His, In all places of His dominion; Bless the LORD, O my soul!*  PS 103:20-22

# *Deeper*
## *From the CD: The Extravagant Love of God*

~~~~~~~~~~~~~~~~~~~~~~~~~~~~~~~~~~~~

Deeper, I wanna go; I wanna go - deeper in you.

Deeper, I wanna go; I wanna go - deeper in you.


As the deer pants for the water,

So my soul longs for deeper in you.

My heart, my mind, my body cry deeper - in you.

In you Oh God, I long to be - deeper in you.

There is a place, a secret place, a hiding place.

That place is deeper in you.

No other love, no greater love.

Is deeper and sweeter than you.


I wanna go; I wanna go - deeper in you.

Yes, I wanna go, I wanna go - deeper in you.

Deep calls unto deep - so take me deeper in you.

Deeper, deeper, yes deeper in you.


A resting place, a hiding place, Jesus in You.

A resting place, a hiding place, Jesus with You.

A resting place, a hiding place, Jesus I need You.

## *Chapter 4*

## The Prophetic Word of God
# What does it mean to seek the Lord?

~~~~~~~~~~~~~~~~~~~~~~~~~~~~~~~~

**Seeking the Lord involves:**

1. Turning to the Lord with the whole heart and in fervent prayer.  Isaiah 55:6

2. Hungering and thirsting for righteousness and God's presence.  Psalms 24:3-6

3. Committing firmly to do God's will and abandoning all actions that offend God.　　　II Chronicles 7:14

4. Believing in and relying on God as your ultimate helper.  Hebrews 13:6

~~~~~~~~~~~~~~~~~~~~~~~~~~~~~~~~

The Lord spoke one morning with a word for His people. He said, *"Tell my people that I want to pour out my spirit on them, but they must seek my face and stop playing with me."*

The Word of the Lord

> *Who may ascend into the hill of the LORD? And who may stand in His holy place?  He who has clean hands and a pure heart, Who has not lifted up his soul to falsehood And has not sworn deceitfully.  He shall receive a blessing from the LORD And righteousness from the God of his salvation. This is the generation of those who seek Him, Who seek Your face—even Jacob. Selah.* PS 24:3-6

## *The Prophetic Word of God*
# The Time is NOW!

~~~~~~~~~~~~~~~~~~~~~~~~~~~~

*The time is now for man to seek Me like never before. The enemy has intensified against My people because the end is drawing near.*

*Those who are not rooted and grounded in Me will be swept away like the chaff which the wind drives away.*

*Do not be concerned with man, stay focused on Me. Look up to Me and not out at man. Stay in My word. The time is here to draw nearer to the Word of God.*

~~~~~~~~~~~~~~~~~~~~~~~~~~~~~~

*If we are to draw from Him all that we need to live the abundant life that He promised His children (John 10:10) - we must live our lives near to God.*

*...I came that they may have life, and have it abundantly.*

The Word of the Lord

## *Take Us In,*

## *Draw Us Into Your Presence.*

# Chapter 5

## What Is True Worship?

~~~~~~~~~~~~~~~~~~~~~~~~~~~~~~~~~~~~~~

True worship is not confined to what we do in church or praise services. Worship is the acknowledgment of God and all His power and glory in everything we do. The highest form of worship is obedience to Him and His Word. To do this, we must know God; we cannot be ignorant of Him. Worship is to glorify and exalt God—to show our loyalty and admiration to our Father.

The Spirit of the Lord is crying, *"Worship Me more."*
*But the hour cometh, and now is, when the true worshippers shall worship the Father in spirit and in truth: for the Father seeketh such to worship him. God is a Spirit: and they that worship him must worship him in spirit and in truth. (John 4:23-24).*

# The Prophetic Word of God
## The Season of Worship

~~~~~~~~~~~~~~~~~~~~~~~~~~~~~~~~~~~

*The season of worship will require a greater and deeper ear to hear. Worship must begin on the inside, it is a matter of the heart.*

*"Deeper" requires a determination to seek Me in ways that the human mind cannot comprehend. It will mean leaving behind the surface way you live for me. When you begin to seek Me in a place where many cannot enter - you will find a depth of me that you will not be able to explain with mere words.*

The Word of the Lord

*...so that Christ may dwell in your hearts through faith; and that you, being rooted and grounded in love, may be able to comprehend with all the saints what is the breadth and length and height and depth, and to know the love of Christ which surpasses knowledge, that you may be filled up to all the fullness of God.* Ephesians 3:17-19

## *The Prophetic Word of God*
# The Season of Worship Is NOW!

~~~~~~~~~~~~~~~~~~~~~~~~~~~~~~~~~~~~~~

In this season of NOW we must begin to live in a place [dimension] in God that goes beyond anything we have ever known. It is not a level it is a dimension. For too long we have tried to stair step or baby step our growth (or faith), but the time is now to begin to move dimensionally in the things of God.

It seems that we penny pinch the Lord when it comes to our blessings. If we have never experienced a move of God in our lives it is difficult to comprehend a move not only in us, but in others as well.

It is for this reason that the people in our lives cannot believe God for His move or blessings. We must silence the voice of defeat that strives to bring us out of dimensional faith.

We cannot afford to allow the voice of unbelief to infiltrate our spirit. We cannot allow the spiritual penny pinchers to cause us to be spiritual penny pinchers.

We must walk in a place that says, "I am ready to receive my inheritance and through my inheritance I can be a vessel that advances the Kingdom of God."

Our attitude should be, "My inheritance will not only bless me, but it will bless others. I will sow into areas that will reap a bountiful harvest."

When the Holy Spirit asks if he can trust us, we must be ready to answer with a resounding yes!! For we must not lie to the Holy Spirit of God. When God can trust us He can use us in great and mighty ways for the Kingdom because He can release the windows of heaven to us.

None of what is given to us is done so that we can live in extravagance - comfort yes, extravagance no.

*Worship begins when you open the door of Your heart to God...*

# *Stop*

# *Wondering &*

# *Wandering &*

# *Start*

# *Standing &*

# *Commanding*

# *Chapter 6*

## *The Prophetic Word of God*
## **A Prepared Place for God**

~~~~~~~~~~~~~~~~~~~~~~~~~~~~~~~~~

*I require a prepared place and a prepared people. I will not manifest my presence anywhere. I must be invited by a people who hunger for my presence.*

*It is not lip service daughter, it is heart service. I delight to dwell in this place [It Is Written Ministries]. It is set aside for Me. The enemy fights you for this place because it belongs to Me. You will not allow anyone to cause my presence to depart. It is precious to me.*

*Know that I do not dwell everywhere - even though I am everywhere. My glory cannot enter a place solely because it calls itself a House of God. There are many churches that do not belong to me. It is a sad day when the church turns its back to me.*

## *The Prophetic Word of God*
# The Essence of His Presence

~~~~~~~~~~~~~~~~~~~~~~~~~~~~~~~~~~~

*As the People begin to understand the essence of My presence and all that it brings to them, they will begin to seek more of me.*

The Word of the Lord

## *The Prophetic Word of God*
# Finding Rest in His Presence

~~~~~~~~~~~~~~~~~~~~~~~~~~~~~~~~~~~

*The rest that man requires to hear Me clearly is often stolen by the enemy. I cannot pour my power into a tired and weakened vessel - weak from the cares of the world. Tired from the business of man made ministry and endeavors. I will pour My power and spirit into a prepared place. A temple capable of carrying my anointing - because my anointing is heavy.*

*You will see more miracles when My people learn to renew their strength in Me. The manifested presence of My glory comes to a vessel prepared solely for Me.*

*My servants and messengers - must hear Me. Learn to rest in Me. If you want to see mighty moves - the move of My presence and glory through your life and ministry, you must learn to truly rest and abide in Me.*

> Yet those who wait for the LORD Will gain new strength; They will mount up with wings like eagles, They will run and not get tired, They will walk and not become weary.  *ISA 40:31*

## *The Prophetic Word of God*
# We are Called to Carry the Light

~~~~~~~~~~~~~~~~~~~~~~~~~~~~~~~~~~~~

I had a dream in which I was standing before the Lord. In His hands He held a cup. I couldn't see all the details of the cup, but I knew He was handing me the cup. He asked the question, *will you drink of this cup?"* Inside the cup I saw His Blood. As I took the cup from Him, I woke up.

Several weeks later in another dream, I was walking down a long hallway carrying a light. The Spirit of the Lord said, *"You have been chosen to carry the Light in these last days."*

I asked the Lord, "Why did you choose me to carry the Light"?  He replied, *"because you were willing to pick it up."*

Webster's dictionary defines the words can and will.  **Can you** means (1) to be able to; (2) ability; (3) to be able to mentally or spiritually; (4) to be able to physically.  **Will you** means (1) choose; (2) willingness; (3) desire.

I was chosen to drink of the cup and carry the light because of the desire in my heart.  Desire comes from a heart that longs to please Him.  Will you carry the light?  Will you drink of the cup?  Will you pick up your cross and follow Him?

---

*He went away a second time and prayed, "My Father, if it is not possible for this cup to be taken away unless I drink it, may your will be done."* Mt 26:42

---

> *This is what the LORD, the God of Israel, said to me: "Take from my hand this cup filled with the wine of my wrath and make all the nations to whom I send you drink it.   When they drink it, they will stagger and go mad because of the sword I will send among them."* [Jer 25:17] *So I took the cup from the LORD'S hand and made all the nations to whom he sent me drink it:* [Jer 25:15-17]

*Worship is a simple thing, it is not difficult or magical, but it must be true.*

## The Press
*From the CD: The Extravagant Love of God*
~~~~~~~~~~~~~~~~~~~~~~~~~~~~~~~~~~~

I press my way into your presence,
I press my way into your courts.
I press my way ….
Oh Lord, Oh Lord of Hosts.

I press my way, yes it's my choice,
Oh how I love to hear your voice.
When I reach for you draw me close.
You are my Lord of Hosts.

I press, I press - It's what I must do.
I press, I press - Because I've got to get to you.
I press, I press.

I've come too far - I won't turn back.
You've seen me through and filled my lack.
I can't wait 'til the day I see your face,
Bless me with you grace.
Through all these tears - The pain I feel.
It works for my good - So I won't fear
Speak to me a word as I draw near.
You are the Lord of Hosts.

I press, I press - It's what I must do.
I press, I press - Because I've got to get to you
I press, I press.

I press, I press - It's what I must do.
I press, I press - Because I've got to get to you
I press, I press.

# *Worship God in the midst of the WAR!*

# Chapter 7

## *The Prophetic Word of God*
## **The Press**

~~~~~~~~~~~~~~~~~~~~~~~~~~~~~~~~

*Do you recall daughter the hunger you felt for Me when I wrote The Press through you?  Your deep desire for me birthed a song that is driving the soul of man to experience the yearning for Me that is inside of you.  The Press is a song of deliverance, freedom, hunger and desire.*

*Always carry the burning within you as you did that day. It is a burning that few will come to experience.  You share your passion for Me through your music and write with a depth of love that grows with each piece you write.*

*The enemy will fight to keep the people out of My presence.  This ministry [It Is Written Ministries] gives them a sanctuary of rest.  I told you this would be a place of refuge.  See how they come and rest?  Teach My people to worship Me.*

The Word of the Lord

When the Lord wrote "The Press" I was on a twenty-one day fast. Half way through I felt I had reached a wall in the spirit and could not press in deeper for more of God. As I was crying out for more He began ministering to me through the words of the song. "The Press" carries a deep passion because I cried out to the Lord and He answered me with a worship song that speaks to the very core of my desire for Him. I did not ask for material things during the fast - I only wanted more of Him.

## *The Prophetic Word of God*
## The Journey for the Press

~~~~~~~~~~~~~~~~~~~~~~~~~~~~~~~~~~~~~

As we begin the journey of pressing into the presence of God, ask yourself:

- ➢ What is it that you desire? Is it His face or His hand?
- ➢ Do you desire His fullness or do you want a spasm of His presence?
- ➢ What happens when He reveals himself?
- ➢ Will you be still before Him or will you talk while He waits to speak?

What man fails to understand is that when we are truly in His presence words have no place.  Flesh cannot stand in His presence - **flesh must die.**

The manifested presence of God requires submission of all that we are.  Isaiah said, *I saw also the Lord sitting upon a throne, high and lifted up, and his train filled the temple* (Isaiah 6:1).  Immediately he (Isaiah) acknowledged his humanness and wretchedness in the manifested presence of God.  When he recognized his sinfulness he had to repent and we must do the same.

When we humble ourselves before El Shaddai - God Almighty, everything we think we are will fall to the ground.  Our titles, positions, jobs, money, fame - will seem like filthy rags.  We will see the futility of trying to be important, powerful, prosperous, etc.  Pride, vanity and the like will fall away.

**What is left?**  An undone creation coming face to face with his Omnipotent, Omniscient and Omnipresent creator.

God can now speak to His creation because all walls and barriers are torn down. When we begin to face our sinfulness, pride, greed and insecurities, God can pull away the layers of fragments and debris to reveal the wretchedness of our sinful nature. We are now in a place where God can use us for Kingdom building.

**Do you want the Lord to use you?** We must not be so busy doing ministry that we miss the reason for ministry. Why does the creation become so engulfed in being busy that we don't take time for the One who wants to bless us?

Busy is busy! God is in our productivity not our busyness. There is no intimacy in busy. When we are in the busyness of our lives we miss intimacy with the Father. Therefore, we miss Him and all that He desires for us.

We also miss the wisdom and knowledge we need to operate in His perfect will. What is His will? Without intimacy you will never know and you will miss Him and all that He has for you.

## The Prophetic Word of God
# We Must Be in Position

~~~~~~~~~~~~~~~~~~~~~~~~~~~~~~~~

*As My Spirit falls, man must be in a spiritual position to receive the outpouring. The position is this: humble, obedient, and in a position of worship. Man misses me because he is not in position. The posture of the heart is very important to Me. A wave of worship must come over the people if they are to receive this outpouring. We must be in position if we are to receive from God that which He has for us.*

The Word of the Lord

*The sacrifices of God are a broken spirit; A broken and a contrite heart, O God, You will not despise.*

*Psalm 51:17*

*For thus says the high and exalted One Who lives forever, whose name is Holy, "I dwell on a high and holy place, And also with the contrite and lowly of spirit In order to revive the spirit of the lowly And to revive the heart of the contrite.*

*Isaiah 57:15*

# Chapter 8

## The Prophetic Word of God
## **Worship in the War**

~~~~~~~~~~~~~~~~~~~~~~~~~~~~~~~~~~~

*As Gideon went into battle, he had no idea who would go with him. He only knew that he had to go. Many around him were not equipped to go.*

*You must understand the Gideon mantle of war. It was when it was down to the wire and it could not be done by man in any way that I [The Lord] could move on behalf of My own.*

*Worship me in the midst of the war. In this season, worship will release the blessings. Worship and obedience move My heart on your behalf.*

*The Word of the Lord*

The Lord gave me a vision of Satan and his manipulative plan against mankind. The Lord showed me a puppet on a string, Satan was the puppet master and we were the puppets. Every time Satan pulled the strings we moved.

No matter how Satan moved us – we followed. Satan said left arm up – arm up. Satan said right arm down – arm down. Close the bible and stop praying – bible closed, prayer ended.

The strings connecting the puppet to the puppet master where strong, in fact the strings were made of reinforced steel. Scissors were useless, cutting shears were broken; in fact nothing man made could cut the strings. It was only with the two edged sword, the Word of God could we be freed from the strings of the puppet master, Satan. Every time we wielded the Word of God, strings broke. In order to keep the bonds broken between Satan and the people of God, we had to stay in constant fellowship and prayer with God our Father.

## The Prophetic Word of God
# *Having done All... Stand*

~~~~~~~~~~~~~~~~~~~~~~~~~~~~~~~~~~

*As you learn to stand in the midst of a battle being waged against you, you will encounter opposition from those closest to you.  You will come to recognize the spirit driving them against you.  You are strong enough to cast out any demons.  Begin to speak and bind the demonic forces that come against you.  The enemy attacks where the links are the weakest.*

*Do you see the doors opening for you?  Unusual doors that no man could or would open for you.  Also see the doors that are closing behind you never to open again.*

*The dream is at hand and all you need to do is walk through the doors.  There will be those who cannot go with you.  I [the Lord] will reveal.*

*Tell My people not to fall into the traps of man, the schemes and gimmicks that man made religion endeavors to use against My sheep.  Tell them it is still a sin of omission and commission when they go along with the doctrines of man and the rudiments of the world. They will stop the flow of blessings in their lives. Tell them to trust Me more than ever. Tell them of the unusual doors I desire to open.*

The Word of the Lord

# The Prophetic Word of God
## Watch and Pray

~~~~~~~~~~~~~~~~~~~~~~~~~~~~~~

*Tell My people the time is NOW more than ever before to watch and pray. For the enemy has sent a storm of demonic delusion to over take the people. Tell the people to watch and pray and to seek Me like never before. Tell them I am listening for their repentance if I am to heal their land.*

*The season is now for their return to Me. There are many that will fall away, but few will return to Me. Tell them of the storm. Tell them to begin to bind the enemy and renounce the demonic forces that stand at the door ready to devour. Tell them.*

The Word of the Lord

*...and My people who are called by My name humble themselves and pray and seek My face and turn from their wicked ways, then I will hear from heaven, will forgive their sin and will heal their land.  " Now My eyes will be open and My ears attentive to the prayer offered in this place. "For now I have chosen and consecrated this house that My name may be there forever, and My eyes and My heart will be there perpetually.* 2CH 7:14-16

# *Keep*

# *Yourself*

# *Full*

# *Of*

# *Holes*

# The Hebrew Names of God
## *From the CD: The Extravagant Love of God*

~~~~~~~~~~~~~~~~~~~~~~~~~~~

*El-Shaddai - Almighty God*

*Jehovah Jireh - The Lord will provide*

*Elohay Kedem - God of the Beginning*

*Jehovah Rohi - The Lord My Shepherd*

*Elohay Kedoshim - Holy God*

*Jehovah Rophe - The Lord our Healer*

*Elohay Elohim - God of Gods*

*Jehovah Tsikenu - The Lord our Righteousness*

*El-Elyon - Most High God*

*Jehovah M'Kaddesh - The Lord Who Sanctifies*

*Jehovah Shammah - The Lord is There*

*Elohay Yishi - God of My Salvation*

*Jehovah Shalom - The Lord our Peace*

*Kadosh - Holy One*

*Jehovah Nissi - The Lord our Banner*

*Elohay Israel - God of Israel*

*Jehovah Sabaoth - The Lord of Hosts*

*El-Olam - Everlasting God*

*Or Ha Olam - Light of the World*

# The Names of Our Lord Jesus Christ
*From the CD: The Extravagant Love of God*

~~~~~~~~~~~~~~~~~~~~~~~~~~~~~~~~~~

*I AM*

*Emmanuel - God with Us*

*Lamb of God*

*Judge*

*Shepherd & Bishop of our Souls*

*Bread of Life*

*Advocate*

*Counselor*

*Prince of Peace*

*Everlasting Father*

*Alpha and Omega*

*Savior*

*Light of the World*

*Rock (Lead me to the Rock that is Higher than I)*

*Forgiver of sins*

*Creator*

*Bridegroom*

*Kinsmen Redeemer*

*The Way, the truth and the Life*

## Chapter 9

*The Prophetic Word of God*
# The Call the Five-Fold Ministry

~~~~~~~~~~~~~~~~~~~~~~~~~~~~~~

The Lord is sending a message to the five-fold ministry. It is a clarion call to wake up and change the way the world views the church through the way we live - as the church. We must come to the realization that souls are at stake. We must stop playing church and stand uncompromisingly on the Word of the Lord.

*The Prophetic Word of God*
# The Call to the Prophet

~~~~~~~~~~~~~~~~~~~~~~~~~~~~~~

*As a prophet of God the standard set for you is high and it is great because you carry My Word. You speak My heart. Many that are called as Prophets of God do not realize the great responsibility that goes with the call. Prophets require a deeper level of intimacy with Me if they are to hear Me clearly. I speak to you in such detail because you stay in My presence. Even though the enemy tries to keep us apart it is mandatory to stay in My presence. Your journey is great as is your destiny, but the intimacy required to walk it out is directly tied to your obedience and intimacy. Each time you answer yes to My will I draw you closer to Me. Tell My people that I am requiring intimacy if they are to carry My vision for their lives.*

The Word of the Lord

## The Prophetic Word of God
# The Call to Leadership

~~~~~~~~~~~~~~~~~~~~~~~~~~~~~~~~~~

*We are entering a season of intense, radical, fellowship with God. This is for leadership. Leaders are falling by the wayside. Demons are attacking leadership by discrediting, discouragement, and through finances.*

*These demons are different, determined, intense and on assignment. We must stay before God in fasting and prayer like never before. Leadership has become an empty pitcher. Intense fellowship will fill the leaders like never before. Revelation like never before will come from intense fellowship. A pouring is happening and it is not all good. Pouring out good and pouring out junk.*

*Leadership will fail if we don't stay connected.*

*There needs to be an insatiable desire to seek the face of God.  An intense level of fellowship.  Until leadership is intense with God we will see more discrediting. Satan is sending a "we want spirit of Fame" over leaders.  To enter into God it is a quest for seeking a new dimension of Him.*

The Word of the Lord through
Be Thou Encourage Ministries
Dr. Margaret Wright

# The Prophetic Word of God
## To Leaders Who Have Fallen Away From the Truth of God's Word

~~~~~~~~~~~~~~~~~~~~~~~~~~~~~~~~~~~

*There is an intense evil waiting to devour them because they did not stay in My presence. It is vital that you [leaders] stay in My presence as I raise you up. The enemy is out to block My voice. They cannot hear me as they slowly fall away from Me.*

*There are those who are out to deceive My sheep and because the sheep are not covered they are being devoured. The enemy can infiltrate a life that is not rooted and grounded in me.*

The Word of the Lord

## The Prophetic Word of God
## To the Money Changers in the House of God

~~~~~~~~~~~~~~~~~~~~~~~~~~~~~~~~~~~~

One morning while in worship the Lord spoke regarding several churches I ministered in recently.

*Take a step back and look at the places I have sent you recently.   Do you see how the church has lost its character and integrity?   Do you see money hungry money changers in the house they call a house of God?*

*Yes, it takes money to do the work, but do you see the schemes and gimmicks they use to manipulate money from the people?   If they  truly trusted in Me, I would open doors and windows for them.*

*They use gimmicks and guilt with no thought for how they make the sheep feel. They have lost the integrity necessary to receive My fullness.  There are many churches that are not Mine.  Many ministers use the church as a way to make a living.  They will strain and drain the sheep so they can live and dress well.*

*Woe unto them that scatter My sheep. There are many ministers that do not hold Me in their hearts. They like the work they do for Me, but they lack the character I require. In the end, they will pay a great price for the blood on their hands.*

The Word of the Lord

## *The Prophetic Word of God* **To the Women of God**

~~~~~~~~~~~~~~~~~~~~~~~~~~~~~~~~~~~~~~~

During a women's conference, the Lord spoke these words for the healing of the women in attendance.

*I am raising women in this season and I require that they begin to address the issues that have beset you. As my vessels of birthing the position I am requiring of you is a position of humility, repentance and obedience. I am raising a remnant of worshippers through women because I am no respecter of persons.*

*Seek me for the issues that are holding you back from your destiny. Hear My word as I lead and guide you into your destiny. Some of the issues you will face are issues that you have hidden deep inside. Hurts, pains and hindrances to My move through you.*

*As I heal you, I will flow through you. I will be your flow. There are old wounds that I will open because they did not heal. You covered them with a band-aid that is not of Me. Allow Me to open the wounds and pour out the poison and begin to mend and heal you.*

The Word of the Lord

# What is worship?

*Any expression*

*of our love to —*

*for who He is,*

*for what He's said,*

*&*

*for what He's doing.*

# Chapter 10

# *Who Is Jesus?*

~~~~~~~~~~~~~~~~~~~~~~~~~~~~~~~~~~~

Jesus presents himself as the "I AM" when challenged by religious leaders.  "I AM" means His is everything.  Jesus came to reveal the God of the Bible and God has revealed himself in His book.  As you learn the names of God you will begin to discover His attributes such as:

Wisdom - Infinitude - Sovereignty - Holiness - Omniscience - Faithfulness - Mercy - Omnipotence - Love - Goodness - Self-sufficiency.

## *Do you know Him or do you know OF Him?*

*When Jesus came into the coasts of Caesarea Philippi, he asked his disciples, saying, Whom do men say that I the Son of man am?  And they said, Some say that thou art John the Baptist: some, Elias; and others, Jeremias, or one of the prophets. He saith unto them, But whom say ye that I am? And Simon Peter answered and said, Thou art the Christ, the Son of the living God.  And Jesus answered and said unto him, Blessed art thou, Simon Bar-jona: for flesh and blood hath not revealed it unto thee, but my Father which is in heaven. And I say also unto thee, That thou art Peter, and upon this rock I will build my church; and the gates of hell shall not prevail against* MT 16:13-18

*In spite of the hardships*

*of my past,*

*God has used everything*

*for my good and His Glory!*

*In fact it was through*

*the hard times,*

*that I grew as*

*a worshipper.*

*Dr. Jacquie*

# The Love of Christ

*...so that Christ may dwell in your hearts through faith; and that you, being rooted and grounded in love, may be able to comprehend with all the saints what is the breadth and length and height and depth, and to know the love of Christ which surpasses knowledge, that you may be filled up to all the fullness of God.*

*Ephesians 3:17-18*

# Chapter 11

## The Prophetic Word of God
### What I Learned Through the Valley of Sickness

~~~~~~~~~~~~~~~~~~~~~~~~~~~~~~~~~~

Over the years I have had a total of five surgeries on my head and breast for cysts and tumors. With each surgery there was a lesson to be learned. Unfortunately, during an illness we can easily take our focus off of God and place it directly on our situation. The illness becomes all about us. We start a pity party on our block and the Lord is not invited. During each illness the Lord walked me through a progressive learning process that drew me closer to Him.

The things I learned through my valley of affliction have given me an insight into the tricks of the enemy that come during illness. It became abundantly clear that sickness is a tool that the enemy will use to draw you away from Jehovah Rophe, the God that Heals Us. Once your focus shifts from the Lord to your situation, the enemy can begin to manipulate your mind with lies, tricks and deceptions. The result, God is not allowed in your healing process and if left unchecked, the fruits of the enemy will begin to take root in your mind, heart and body.

While going through my finasurgeriesl , the doctor informed me that I had cysts in my head and a tumor in my breast. She believed the breast tumor was cancerous, but not the cysts in my head. She went on to say that I needed to have two surgeries, but the human body could not withstand the trauma of two surgeries of this magnitude. Therefore, I had to decide which surgery to have performed first.

My finite mind could not rap itself around the severity of my situation and I submerged myself into a bottle of cognac and stayed there for three days. As day three approached, I was at the bottom of the pit and the enemy knew it was time to strike. Subtly and cautiously the enemy approached me and whispered: *"You know that you must have two surgeries, don't you? You also know that there is cancer in your body, don't you? You do know that there is no one to care for you, don't you? The cancer is going to ravage your body and you will waste away in pain and agony. Your only solution is to take your life now and spare yourself the pain of cancer and surgery.*" When you are at your weakest most vulnerable point, the enemy, Satan will step in and fire a missile directly at your mind. He spoke clearly to a woman full of alcohol because my mind and spirit were open in the worst way.

At the moment I was contemplating suicide it was also the moment the Lord would step in. There was so much pain inside of me that I could not fight, to be perfectly honest, I didn't know how to fight. I remember crying out with a force from deep inside as I rolled out of bed and onto the floor, crying out for help from the Father. It was at that moment that the Lord lifted Satan off my back, and gave me a moment to make a decision. I cried out, "please help me, Jesus."

The Lord replied, *"All sickness is not unto death, fight."* Instantly, strength arose from within and I began to pray. Lying on the floor, I cried out to the Lord and He heard me and delivered me from the hand of the enemy.

The more I prayed the stronger I felt. The stronger I felt the more I fought. The bible tells us in Zechariah 4:6 that it is *not by might, nor by power, but by my spirit, saith the LORD of hosts.* The Spirit of the Lord filled the room and gave me the strength to fight.

I asked the Lord which surgery to have first and He instructed me to have the breast surgery performed first. The full healing process took approximately nine months after which I had the fifth surgery for the cysts in my head.

The lessons I learned during the journey through the valley of the shadow of sickness will be with me for the rest of my life. If you receive nothing else from this, please know - The Lord is with you through every trial and tribulation. He is right there to lead and guide you through the valley of... He loves you and desires the best for you. Your wisdom and strength to endure will come from your journey through the valley of the shadow of...

Each of us will walk through our valleys differently and we will come away with wisdom, strength and knowledge that we can share with others. We are overcomers by the Blood of the Lamb and by the word of our testimonies.

*What I Learned Through the Valley of Sickness:*

- ➢ I learned how easily man can stray away from the presence of God.
- ➢ Sickness is a tool the enemy will use to draw you away from Jehovah Rophe, the God that Heals Us.
- ➢ We become focused on our circumstances and we forget to worship God.
- ➢ The enemy will keep you focused on YOU and there is no room for God.
- ➢ The fruits of the enemy can take root in your mind, heart and body.
- ➢ When you are at your weakest, the enemy will fire missiles directly at your mind.
- ➢ When you are at your weakest, the Lord is also there to deliver you.
- ➢ Though you walk through the valley of the shadow of… *The Lord is with you if you allow Him to carry you through.*

➢ During the fifth surgery, The Lord said, *"Why is it that you worship Me when things are good, but you don't worship when things are going wrong?"*

➢ Worship will ease the pain in your body because you commit the body to the One who created it.

➢ Worship the Lord in spite of the physical pain and He will show you an awesome move of God. Sing, pray, moan, wave your hand... worship begins in the heart.

*The Prophetic Word of God*
# Taking Authority over Sickness

~~~~~~~~~~~~~~~~~~~~~~~~~~~~~~~~~~

One morning I awoke with a headache due to sleeping in an uncomfortable position. Suddenly the pressure from the headache increased with a great intensity and the Lord spoken these words:

*You have the power to speak to any situation, but because of the cares of the world you have allowed it to diminish My power in you. You could at any moment lay hands on the back of your neck and speak to the pain in My Name and it would leave you. You still do not realize the power within you.*

Because of the trials and situations we face each day, we can become so involved in the battle that we forget we are warriors and walk in the power Jesus Christ has given us. Power over any mountain. When we speak to the mountain we must not doubt in any way. Holy boldness must be in every word we speak. Jesus gave us authority to heal the sick, raise the dead and cast out demons.

In the new season in which we are walking, we must take authority at every turn and not waiver nor doubt. Fear and unbelief have no place in the warfare.

Final note: I laid my hand on the back of my neck and took authority in the Name of Jesus and the pain left.

## *The Prophetic Word of God*
# We must stay in Balance

~~~~~~~~~~~~~~~~~~~~~~~~~~~~~~~~~~~~

Maintaining balance in our lives is essential. It is an integral part of our physical, mental and emotional health. While going through my surgeries for cysts and tumors it was the enemy's goal to keep me off balance. The words

The Lord spoke regarding balance in our lives give us a road map to recognizing the enemy's tactics against us.

*The enemy will try to keep you off balance by constantly throwing darts, missiles or grenades at you. Shifting the focus is the enemy's goal, he is on a search and destroy mission.*

*He is attempting to take the focus off your relationship with Jesus and put the focus on you. Every time he launches a fiery dart your focus shifts to you and the situation you are facing. It is like walking a tight rope, but don't look down - look up and keep your balance and focus on Jesus, the hope of glory.*

*We must begin each day by binding the enemy. Commanding him back to the abyss or hell and releasing the peace of God. We must take authority over every demonic force that would try to come against us. This means beginning your day with prayer.*

The Word of the Lord

# Who are you fighting against?

*For we wrestle not against flesh and blood, but against principalities, against powers, against the rulers of the darkness of this world, against spiritual wickedness in high places. Wherefore take unto you the whole armour of God that ye may be able to withstand in the evil day, and having done all, to stand. Stand therefore, having your loins girt about with truth, and having on the breastplate of righteousness; And your feet shod with the preparation of the gospel of peace; Above all, taking the shield of faith, wherewith ye shall be able to quench all the fiery darts of the wicked. And take the helmet of salvation, and the sword of the Spirit, which is the word of God: Praying always with all prayer and supplication in the Spirit, and watching thereunto with all perseverance and supplication for all saints. Ephesians 6:12-18*

# Chapter 12

## The Prophetic Word of God
## *Time Alone with God*

~~~~~~~~~~~~~~~~~~~~~~~~~~~~~~~~

What is the secret to maintaining a living connection with God? The answer is daily communion with Him. It is the number one priority of the Christian life. Daily communion with God is the key that opens every spiritual door.

Abiding with God is simply fellowshipping with Him. We must stay in touch with God, talking to God and listening for God. The Bible says in John 15:7: *"If you abide in Me, and My words abide in you, ask whatever you wish, and it will be done for you."*

In order to know God we must spend time alone with Him. Time is the one element in our lives that once it's gone we can never get it back. As we grow in our relationship with the Lord our time with Him becomes more precious.

Have you ever gotten up at 3 a.m. to spend time with the Lord? My 3 a.m. wake up calls brings a smile to my face because it's my Father gently nudging me to get out of bed to come spend time with Him. Time alone with God is precious - just Father and child, talking, praying, singing, laughing, crying and enjoying every moment together. When God awakens you rest assure that you are waking up to God's peace surrounding you. Communing with God is not a project - it is a lifestyle. Spending time with Him and time in His Word must be a way of life.

If we want the fullness of God, we can't run to Him when we're in trouble or when the road is rough. To make matters worse we run to Him with our hands out for what He can give us and never up in worship to Him. You will never receive His fullness like that. Instead, we must seek God daily in prayer and in His Word. We must seek God when things are up and when things are down. We must live to know God. James 4:3 says, *"Draw near to God and He will draw near to you."*

When you are alone - who do you spend time with? When you need someone to talk to - who do you call on? Have you ever called a friend and got their voice mail or answering machine when you really needed to talk to them? When you call on God you will never hear: *"hello, this is God. I'm away from the throne right now, but leave me a message and I'll get back to you. Peace be with you."*

God is always there for you. He loves you and wants to spend time with you. Give God the best of your time, the best of your love and the best of everything. Then you will experience the extravagance of His love.

---

> *If ye abide in me, and my words abide in you, ye shall ask what ye will, and it shall be done unto you.* Jn 15:7

# The Prophetic Word of God
## *Seek My Face*

~~~~~~~~~~~~~~~~~~~~~~~~~~~~~~~~~~~~

➤ The Spirit of the Lord said, *tell My people that I want to pour out My Spirit on them, but they must seek My face and stop playing with me."*

➤ *Take My people deeper into Me. Tell My people that I love them and I am calling for their obedience if I am to heal their land.*

➤ *Tell My people, I am here for them in all that they do. Trust me even more.*

<div align="right">The Word of the Lord</div>

## The Prophetic Word of God
## *Make Time for God*

~~~~~~~~~~~~~~~~~~~~~~~~~~~~~~~~~~~~~

The Word of the Lord regarding fasting and our daily routines. The Spirit of the Lord said, *"We [mankind] have compacted so much into our everyday life that we have left little room for Him. Three day, seven day, fourteen day and twenty-one day fasts that are singularly inclusive of Him are nearly impossible.*

*We fast food, sex, television, etc. but for the mot part we continue the other compacted activities of our daily lives. Therefore, the chance for an encounter, a lengthy encounter with Him are in reality stolen moments.*

*Although we fast for more of God, we are in fact robbing ourselves of the most exciting chance to be with God. Daily routines are just that - daily regiments of agendas. We are programmed by life and not by God. For the most part we have a very rigid agenda call life.*

*There is so much that I [the Lord] want to give my children, but they give so little of themselves to Me.*

*Where is the sacrifice? When man begins to de-clutter his life, then he can make room for Me.*

*The things man calls ministry are often agendas used to make man feel as if he is doing it for My Kingdom. When in fact he has no idea of the true direction I want him to take. But because it seems right in his human eye, he goes about his business while leaving Mine unattended.*

*Intimacy with Me is not occasional, it is a lifestyle. There is a way that seem right to man... The church has not only failed the people, but it has also failed Me. I am beginning to raise men and women that know Me intimately and will stand for Me.*

*Do not concern yourselves with those that claim positions of leadership because most of them I did not chose. You will see those that are great in the eyes of man begin to fall. Do not be surprised or amazed because I told you I was going to pull the covers back and expose the filthy and vile things they are doing in My Name. Remember Ezekiel?*

*The abominations will continue to grow, but they have only just begun.  Because man has strayed from me in his heart.  There are those who have distanced themselves from Me believing they are doing My work, praying with an empty heart and lying to themselves.*

*I hold the church accountable because they have lost intimacy with Me and therefore cannot teach the people intimacy.  Each Sunday they crowd into buildings where I am not welcome.  They sing to a God they do not know.  They pray to a God that does not hear them.*

*Until the leadership is humble and broken the people will remain indifferent to Me.  Many of them walk in cloaks of false humility - deceiving the sheep.  They are slaughtering my lambs.*

*Man must learn to break the constraints life has placed on them.  This is the only way you will know and understand a deeper intimacy with Me.*

*As I guide you day by day, there will be many things you do not understand, but know that they are for your good.*

*It is necessary for where I desire to take you.  Through this your obedience to me will grow.*

*Tell My people to clean up their lives so there is room for me.  The house must be clean; I will not dwell in an unclean thing.  It is time to go deeper into Me.*

## *A Treasure in the Pleasure of Loving God*
### *From the CD:  The Extravagant Love of God*
~~~~~~~~~~~~~~~~~~~~~~~~~~

*There's a treasure in the pleasure of loving God.*
*Yes, a treasure in the pleasure of loving my God.*

*There's a treasure in the pleasure, Lord I can't measure.*

*There's a treasure in the pleasure of loving God.*

*As deep as an ocean,  As wide as the sea.*

*The secrets of your love are endless,*

*It's a joy unto me.*

*As your love covers…*

*Your grace and mercy set me free.*

*There's a treasure, that you cannot measure,*

*There's a treasure in the pleasure of loving God.*

*The light of your love shines brightly.*

*I feel you close to me*

*Jesus you died for me.*

*There's a treasure in the pleasure…*

*How can I measure?*

*No love can compare…*

*The deeper it grow, Your love clearly shows.*

*I found a treasure, when I discovered the pleasure of*

*loving my God.*

*As a teacher it is my passion to teach the people of God to worship God. There is no formula, that says, this is how you worship, but there is a position of the heart that God requires from us and that is where worship must begin...*

*IN YOUR HEART.*

*Chapter 13*

## The Prophetic Word of God
### *The Nails He Bore for Us*

~~~~~~~~~~~~~~~~~~~~~~~~~~~~~~

Recently at Thursday night Encountering God Prayer the Lord began to speak to us about the nails that He bore for us *(1. make deep hole in something: to make a deep, neatly formed hole such as one made by a drill or a bullet. 2. Penetrate: to penetrate into the inner or hidden parts of somebody or something).* He instructed me to take the nails from the altar and give one to each person. During worship He spoke these words:

*The nail that you hold in your hand is only a representation of what I bore for mankind. If man truly understood what I endured, he would desire more of Me.*

*The time is coming and now is when man will be drawn away from Me. They will follow seducing spirits that will lead them astray. The remnant that remains in Me will experience an outpouring of My love, My presence and My blessings. The fallen will not understand, but they will envy, hate, and strive to tear down what I have built*

91

*through My remnant. But they will fail because no weapon formed against those that belong to Me will prosper.*

*You will begin to see the lost that are tired of man made religion begin to come. They will come slowly, but they will come. Stay in My presence and do not doubt.*

**The Word of the Lord.**

*Who his own self bare our sins in his own body on the tree, that we, being dead to sins, should live unto righteousness: by whose stripes ye were healed.*

(1Peter 2:24 KJV)

*He himself bore our sins in his body on the tree, so that we might die to sins and live for righteousness; by his wounds you have been healed.*

(1Peter 2:24 NIV)

*...and He Himself bore our sins in His body on the cross, so that we might die to sin and live to righteousness; for by His wounds you were healed.*

(1 Peter 2:24 NASB).

*He personally bore our sins in His [own] body on the tree [as on an altar and offered Himself on it], that we might die (cease to exist) to sin and live to righteousness. By His wounds you have been healed.*

(1 Peter 2:24 Amplified)

If we could grasp within our finite minds the depths of the love of God for His people, in that Jesus bore our sins so that we would have the right to eternal life, maybe we wouldn't take the life He gave us for granted. When we decide that we will no longer live on the surface of Christianity, then we will begin to call out for more of His presence. This means that we will not settle for cookie cutter worship, milk toast messages and name it and claim it blessings. 1 Peter 2:24 and Isaiah 53:5 will become the foundation for healing and wholeness in every aspect of our lives.

If we took Isaiah 53:5 to heart we would come to realize that: *he was wounded for our transgressions,* and we would take the wounds He received more seriously. *He was bruised for our iniquities,* and we would acknowledge the depths of our sinful nature. *The*

93

*chastisement of our peace was upon him* and there was and is no one on the face of the earth that could redeem us and the peace of all mankind was on His shoulders. *With his stripes we are healed* - healed from sickness, disease, poverty, bondage and the like.

Wisdom is the key to a renewed mind. A renewed mind is the beginning to change in our lives. A changed life is the beginning of growth. Without wisdom we will continue to walk in darkness and defeat. *Wisdom is the principal thing; therefore get wisdom: and with all thy getting get understanding.* (Proverbs 4:7).

Theses are the word the Lord spoke regarding wisdom and understanding. He said, *"In some things understanding cannot come if we do not seek growth through wisdom that comes from above. The carnal mind cannot understand the things of God. Man must leave his surface way of thinking if he is to go to the depths of Me."*

Deep calls unto deep. The depths of the true and living God are calling us to a deeper place in Him. *As the deer pants for the water brooks, so my soul pants for You, O*

*God. My soul thirsts for God, for the living God.*

Psalm 42:1-2

This is the cry of a thirsty soul. Is your inner man crying out for more of God? Do you find yourself longing for more of God? After you have heard the Word of God, do you find yourself longing for more? Are you experiencing staleness in your worship? Have you found praise to be repetitious? Do you go to church to praise the praise team and worship the worship leaders? If you answered yes to any of these questions, your soul may be longing to go deeper. *Why are you in despair, O my soul? And why have you become disturbed within me? Hope in God, for I shall again praise Him For the help of His presence* (PS 42:5). Your faith and hope might be placed in the wrong thing or the wrong person.

The Lord is ready to ease the pains of life. We need to turn it over to Him. *My flesh and my heart faileth: but God is the strength of my heart, and my portion for ever.* (Psalm 73:26). Is God the strength of your heart and your portion? If so, then He is ALL that you need to conquer any battle that is waged against you. We must be like King David when he was in the cave and crying out to God:

*I cry aloud with my voice to the LORD; I make supplication with my voice to the LORD. I pour out my complaint before Him; I declare my trouble before Him. When my spirit was overwhelmed within me, You knew my path. In the way where I walk they have hidden a trap for me. Look to the right and see; for there is no one who regards me; there is no escape for me; No one cares for my soul. I cried out to You, O LORD; I said, "You are my refuge, my portion in the land of the living. "Give heed to my cry, For I am brought very low; deliver me from my persecutors, For they are too strong for me. " Bring my soul out of prison, So that I may give thanks to Your name; The righteous will surround me, For You will deal bountifully with me* (Ps 142:1-7). Do you long for God the way David did when he was in the wilderness of Judah, *O God, You are my God; I shall seek You earnestly; My soul thirsts for You, my flesh yearns for You, In a dry and weary land where there is no water.*

*Thus I have seen You in the sanctuary, To see Your power and Your glory. Because Your loving kindness is better than life, My lips will praise You. So I will bless You as long as I live; I will lift up my hands in Your name. (Ps. 63:1-4).*

When you get to this point in your relationship with the Lord you will know that your soul is longing for more of God and deeper into God. Your surface Christianity is by the wayside and you are on the journey to a more intimate relationship with Him.

You are about to walk through a door that leads to the extravagant love of God. Enjoy the journey...

## Extravagant Love of God
*From the CD: The Extravagant Love of God*
~~~~~~~~~~~~~~~~~~~~~~~~~~~~~~~~~~~~~

More precious than gold,

Sweeter than the honeycomb.

Its flames are flames of fire,

Burning through my heart.

The extravagant love of God.


Your love grows deeper with each breath.

And covers every sin sick step.

Your love covers like morning dew.

The extravagant love of God.

A love so intoxicating and exhilarating

Has finally captured my heart.

A love that's deeper than any ocean.

The extravagant love of God.


Your love upholds me

As it unfolds around me.

You are mine and I am yours.

*Mmmm...* The extravagant love of God.

You have ravished my heart,

With the fragrance of your love.

My heart beats for you

As My body yearns for…

The extravagant love of God.

Set as a seal upon my heart,

Shower down your love…

Guide me to the Secret Place

And the shelter of your arms

Waters cannot quench this love

Nor floods drench its fire.

What would man give for a taste of **THIS LOVE**?

For the extravagant love of God.

Yes, the extravagant love of God.

I found the extravagant love of God.

# Chapter 14

## *The Prophetic Word of God*
# The Extravagance of God's Love
~~~~~~~~~~~~~~~~~~~~~~~~~~~

**Extravagant:  abundant: existing or produced in quantity**
* *Extravagant praise*
* *Extravagant love*

**Agape (Love):  selfless love felt by Christians for their fellow human beings; love that is wholly selfless and spiritual**

The Extravagance of God's love towards us is so deep it is endless, so wide it is limitless, and so high it reaches infinity.  When the hunger within us begins to burn with intensity like never before - it will literally consume your heart.

The desire for more of "His manifested presence" will birth a press in you that becomes insatiable.  It will only be satisfied when you abide in His presence.

*...that you, being rooted and grounded in love, may be able to comprehend with all the saints what is the*

*breadth and length and height and depth, and to know the love of Christ which surpasses knowledge, that you may be filled up to all the fullness of God.*

*Ephesians 3:18-19*

## The Prophetic Word of God
### Experience the Extravagance of the Love of God

~ ~ ~ ~ ~ ~ ~ ~ ~ ~ ~ ~ ~ ~ ~ ~ ~ ~ ~ ~ ~ ~ ~ ~ ~ ~ ~

When we think of love we often consider the love between man and woman, parent and child, friend to friend. There is no love more extravagant than the love that the Creator has for His creation. The love of God for His people is a love that could never be described within the pages of any book except the Holy Bible. The only words that come close are found in the Word of God: *"For God so loved the world that He gave His only begotten Son, that whosoever believes in Him should not perish but have everlasting life."* (John 3:16)

The finite mind of man cannot begin to grasp the infinite love God. My desire through this book and worship CD is to follow the mandate given by the Lord. The mandate: *"teach my people to worship Me and tell them of My love.*" I pray that as you read this book and\or listen to the music the glory of the Lord will shine through and your relationship with the Him will be magnified as you go to a new level in Him.

I pray that your love relationship with Our Lord and Savior grows as you feel the passion of a heart burning for our Heavenly Father and His only begotten Son, Jesus Christ. The Lord spoke these words as I heard The Extravagant Love of God for the first time, "*You are describing My Love.*" Experience the Extravagant Love of God. My heart beats for... and my body yearns for - *The Extravagant Love of God.*

*The Prophetic Word of God*
# Conclusion - Growing Deeper
~~~~~~~~~~~~~~~~~~~~~~~~~~~

The Lord desires to use the elements of your past and present to take you to another level in Him. We should not allow the past or the present to hinder our growth. It is through the trying of our faith that we are made stronger and wiser.

We are soldiers for Christ and if we are to stand for what is right, avoid playing games and run the race in an uncompromising stance - we will come to realize that although the adversities of life will try to overtake us, *NO weapon formed against us shall prosper.* The Word of God did not say it would not form, the Word of God says it will not prosper in your life.

As we go through, we must know that worship is our best weapon in the midst of the warfare. Ninjas have stealth like moves; armies have guns; and believers have worship. It is through our worship that our victory is sure. The enemy often looks like he is winning, never the less, *NO weapon formed against you shall prosper.*

The enemy will try to discourage worship in order to keep you out of the presence of God.  It is in the presence of the Lord that you will find peace, joy, love, contentment, victory and answers to your questions.

If we are to live a victorious life and experience the extravagance of God's love, we must address our spiritual priorities.  In order to experience the extravagance of His love we must learn to walk in victory.  Learning to walk in victory means that we address key issues that effect our focus, faith, and source of power.  Without the proper focus we will continually get off course.  I refuse to be a victim in any aspect of my life.  The Lord calls us to be victors through the blood of the Lamb of God.  Therefore, we need to understand what elements shape a victorious life and the elements that lead us to defeat.

*What elements shape a victorious life?*

A victorious life says:

1. FOCUS: Lord Jesus Christ (John 14:6)
2. OBJECT OF FAITH: Cross of Christ (Ro. 6:3-5)
3. POWER SOURCE: Holy Spirit (Ro. 8:1-2, 11)
4. RESULTS: Victory ( Ro. 6:14)

It would be unfair to give you the positive side of a victorious life and omit the way most believers live:

1. FOCUS: Works
2. OBJECT OF FAITH: Performance
3. POWER SOURCE: Self
4. RESULTS: Defeat

➤ Are you focused on the Lord or your works for the Lord?

➤ Is the object of your faith the Cross of Christ or how you perform for Christ?

➤ Is your power source the Holy Spirit or your *self* spirit?

➤ What are the results of your efforts in life: victory or defeat?

In taking a spiritual inventory of your lifestyle you will be able to see if you are walking in victory or defeat. If you can answer yes to any of the next questions, it will be a major step in discovering who God meant for you to be. Are you living a victorious life? Are you experiencing the extravagance or the fullness of God's blessings? Do you experience the *"I don't why God is not blessing me"* blues?

II Chronicles 7:14-15 tells us, *if my people, who are called by my name, will humble themselves and pray and seek my face and turn from their wicked ways, then will I hear from heaven and will forgive their sin and will heal their land. Now my eyes will be open and my ears attentive to the prayers offered in this place.* We must be in a position of humility and obedience to the Lord if we are to receive His blessings.

*Take a look at several steps that will help you move toward a deeper more intimate relationship with the Lord.*

- ➢ **Return to God** - We must humble ourselves, pray and seek the face of God. (II Chronicles 7:14).

- ➢ **Have faith in God** - Our faith should be simple and pure, like the attitude of a child.

- ➢ **Fear not** - God has not given us the spirit of fear, but of power, love and a sound mind. (2 Timothy 1:7).

- ➢ **Put on the full armor of God** - Be strong with the Lord's mighty power. (Ephesians 6:10-18).

- ➢ **God's call for intimacy** - God is calling us to intimacy with Him.

- ➢ **Worship** - Worship God in Spirit and in Truth. Glorifying Him with a heart that's pure. (Psalm 51:10; John 4:23-24).

- ➢ **Give all glory to God** - He is glorified through His creation, His son Jesus, and believers who are living for Him.  Give God Glory in all that you do.

- ➢ **Find joy in everyday life** - Whenever trouble comes your way, let it be an opportunity for joy.  The joy of the Lord is your strength. (Nehemiah 8:10).

- ➢ **Pass your test** - When your faith is tested, your endurance grows.

- ➢ **Know that God is in control** - God is in control and He loves you. He knows what's best for you. (Jeremiah 29:11).

- ➢ **Trust God**-Trust in God's plan for your life. (Pro 3:5)

# Grow Deeper!!

## ...For my soul follows hard after thee.

## *Prayer of Salvation*

~~~~~~~~~~~~~~~~~~~~~~~~~~~~~~~~

No matter what you do in life, nothing else will matter except your relationship with Jesus Christ. A committed relationship with Jesus is the key to a victorious life. Our Lord and Savior laid down His life for us. He rose again for us so that we could spend eternity with Him. Jesus said, *"I am come that they might have life, and that they might have it more abundantly."*

It is God's will that everyone receive eternal salvation. The only way to receive salvation is to call upon the name of Jesus and confess Him as Lord of your life. The Bible says in Romans 10:9-13, *that if thou shalt confess with thy mouth the Lord Jesus, and shalt believe in thine heart that God hath raised him from the dead, thou shalt be saved. For with the heart man believeth unto righteousness; and with the mouth confession is made unto salvation. For the scripture saith, whosoever believeth on him shall not be ashamed. For there is no difference between the Jew and the Greek: for the same Lord over all is rich unto all that call upon him. For whosoever shall call upon the name of the Lord shall be saved.*

God loves you, no matter who you are, no matter what your past. God loves you so much that He gave His one and only begotten Son for you. The Bible tells us *"...whoever believes in him shall not perish but have eternal life"* (John 3:16 NIV). Jesus laid down His life and rose again so that we could spend eternity with Him in heaven and experience His absolute best on earth. If you would like to receive Jesus into your life, say the following prayer aloud. It is vital that you mean it from your heart.

> **Heavenly Father, I come to You admitting that I am a sinner. Right now, I choose to turn away from sin, and I ask You to cleanse me of all unrighteousness. I believe that Your Son, Jesus, died on the cross to take away my sins. I also believe that He rose again from the dead so that I may be justified and made righteous through faith in Him. I call upon the name of Jesus Christ to be the Savior of my life. Jesus, I choose to follow You, and I ask that You fill me with the power of**

*the Holy Spirit. I declare right now that I am a born-again child of God. I am free from sin, and full of the righteousness of God. I am saved in Jesus' name. Amen.*

If you prayed this prayer to receive Jesus Christ as your Lord and Savior or if this book has blessed your life, we would like to hear from you. Please write us:

Igniting the Fire Publishing
1314 North 38th Street, Suite 101
Kansas City, KS  66102
**Or**
It Is Written Ministries
1314 North 38th Street, Suite 102
Kansas City, KS  66102

## Meet Dr. Jacquie

### The Author

Dr. Jacquelyn Brown-Hadnot is an author and teacher whose passion is to teach the bible in a way that changes lives. She has written several books such as the award winning *Cry Aloud, Spare Not! A Prophetic Call to the Fast God Has Chosen for You*, which received the 2007 Indie Excellence Finalist Award and USA Book News 2006 Best General Religion Book of the Year; Cry Aloud, Spare Not! The Companion Study Guide; His Mercy Endures Forever: Psalms, Prayers & Meditations for the Heart; To Make War with the Saints: Satan's Kingdom Agenda; A Treasure in the Pleasure of Loving God and many print and audio books.

### The Pastor

It is her great love for the Body of Christ that prompted Jacquie to birth It Is Written Ministries, Inc. It Is Written Ministries is a unique non-profit ministry that endeavors to encourage, motivate, and educate individuals to walk in wisdom, character, and holiness. It Is Written feeds the triune man; mind, body and spirit through outreaches such as food and clothing pantries, nursing home outreaches, meals to the homeless and teaching ministries on foundations for victorious Christian living, biblical financial principles, prayer and worship.

She holds a Doctorate in Pastoral Theology, a Masters in Ministry Leadership and Bachelors in Theology.

## The Teacher / Speaker

Dr. Jacquie is a frequently requested speaker for churches, women's groups, general audiences, and seminars for independent gospel artists, biblical financial principals, fasting, prayer and worship.

She is the founder of the Agape Learning Center, an outreach of It Is Written Ministries.  The learning center was founded to provide a quality education to individuals with a desire to grow in their personal lives, but cannot afford a traditional educational system.

Jacquie has also made television appearances on such shows as Lift Him up Kansas, TBN Praise The Lord,

Soldiers for Jesus Christ, Joy Night Television and several others.

She is also the host of *Light for Your Path* and *The Heart of a Psalmist* radio broadcasts that air nationally and internationally in more than 56 countries, 80+ cities.

She has also been a guest on radio shows, including The Joy of Gospel, Let's Talk Honestly, XM Radio, Gospel Spotlight, The Virtuous Women's Literary Corner, and Legacy Alive! and many others.

## The Psalmist

Jacquie flows under a powerful three-fold evangelistic, psalmist and prophetic anointing causing her to be an effective vessel for the Kingdom of God. Jacquie is a Spoken Word Psalmist and her CD "His Mercy Endures Forever" has received nationwide airplay, 2006 Newsome Award for Spoken Word of the Year, 2005 Joy Night Music Award for Best Worship Music, 2005 Omer Award for Spoken Word of the Year, 2006 Momentum Award nomination and 2006 Just Plain Folks nomination. She has released two additional worship projects, The Spoken

Word of Love and The Extravagant Love of God.

Jacquie frequently ministers music where she speaks. As a psalmist music is a vital part of worship. Jacquie uses music as a way to connect to the heart of God's people.

## The Entrepreneur

Jacquie and her husband Minister Gregory Hadnot launched Igniting the Fire Media Group in 2006 which includes:

➢ ITF Publishing
➢ ITF Records
➢ GLORI Radio
➢ ITF Television

Jacquie has been the President and CFO of The Diversified Group, Inc. an accounting and income preparation firm for over twenty five years.

Jacquie and Minister Gregory have been married for over nine years and together they oversee It Is Written Ministries. They reside in Overland Park, KS. She has one daughter, Jacquanda and a grandson, Tristan.

## Other Books & Materials by Dr. Jacquie

~~~~~~~~~~~~~~~~~~~~~~~~~~~~~~~~~~~

# Books in Print

- ➢ Cry Aloud, Spare Not! A Prophetic Call to the Fast God Has Chosen

- ➢ Cry Aloud, Spare Not! The Companion-Study Guide

- ➢ His Mercy Endures Forever: Psalms, Prayers & Meditations

- ➢ To Make War with the Saints; Satan's Kingdom Agenda

- ➢ A Treasure in the Pleasure of Loving God

- ➢ Loving God through His Names: 365 Days of the Year

- ➢ Closing the Doors to Satan's Attacks: *Overcoming Fear*

- ➢ Where Is Your God? Have We Lost the Referential Fear of the Lord?

# Audio Books & Teachings

- ➢ More of You… (Volume 1) April 2010

- ➢ In the Face of Adversity: *Overcoming Life's Storms*

- ➢ Be Not Deceived…

- ➢ Where Is Your God?

- ➢ Recognizing Your Due Season

- ➢ Praying the Healing Scriptures

- ➢ The Enemy in Me: *Overcoming Self-Life Issues*

# Music

- ➢ The Extravagant Love of God (March 2010)

- ➢ His Mercy Endures Forever: Praying the Psalms

- ➢ The Spoken Word of Love

**For More Information:**
www.jacquiehadnot.com
www.ignitingthefire.net

www.ingramcontent.com/pod-product-compliance
Lightning Source LLC
Chambersburg PA
CBHW061959040426
42447CB00010B/1824